INTRODUCTION TO CONTRACT LAW IN INDIA

SIVA PRASAD BOSE

This book is dedicated to the constitution of India, which is the source from which all laws in India derive.

Contents

Preface

Contract Law is an important branch of law that governs contracts. They are essential to most or all commercial transactions.

In this book, we discuss what is a contract, the history of contract law and the important laws in India that govern contracts, namely the Indian contract act and the sale of goods act. We also discuss the conditions for a valid or invalid contract, the elements of a contract and some special types of contracts.

It is hoped that this book might help interested people to become familiar with contract law in India.

Acknowledgements

While writing this book, we have gone through the following sources related to contract laws:

LexisNexis. Mulla. The Indian Contract Act by Dindhaw Fardunji Mulla. Edition 2021

Encyclopedia Britannica. Contract law. https://www.britannica.com/topic/contract-law

John D Calamari and JM Perillo. Contracts. Black Letter Outlines, Fifth edition. Thomson Reuters.

CHAPTER ONE

What is Contract Law?

In this chapter, we will discuss the concept of contracts and contract law in brief.

1.1 What is a contract

A contract is a voluntary agreement between two or more persons to exchange something of value. It confers certain rights and imposes certain obligations to the parties making the contract, which are enforceable by law. In a contract, each person is legally bound to do what is promised. A party who fails to live up to the agreed promise has breached the contract.

When we agree to buy something, we essentially form a legal contract. For example, A buying a bar of soap from B upon making a payment of Rs 10 is a contract of sale. The law of contract is relevant for many parts of our daily life, and it is important to understand contracts in order to protect ourselves as consumers.

A contract between two parties is marked with one party making an offer and the other party giving their assent to the offer. The offer made may alternatively be rejected by the other party, or a counteroffer made, whose acceptance will create another legally binding contract.

Contract law deals with the definition of a contract, elements of a contract, validity and duration of the contract, the consequences if any party breaks the contract and similar issues. In India, contract law is served by the Sale of Goods Act 1930 and by the Indian Contract Act 1872.

1.2 Meaning of contract

The meaning of contract, taken from different sources, is as follows:

- An agreement enforceable by law is a contract: Indian contract Act 1872
- An enforceable covenant or agreement between two or more persons with a lawful consideration or course (Tomlin)

- From dictionary of finance and investment: Contract in general is an agreement by which right or acts are exchanged for lawful consideration. to be valid, it must be entered into by competent parties, must cover a legal and moral transaction, must possess mutuality and must represent a meeting of moods. countless transactions in finance and investments are covered by contracts.
- While it is probably impossible to give an absolute and universally correct definition of a contract, the most accepted definition is a promise or a set of promises which the law will enforce. The expression "contract" may be used to describe any or all the following:

a. the series of promises or acts themselves constituting the contract
b. the document or documents constituting the contract
c. the document or documents constituting or evidencing that series or promises or acts or their performance
d. the legal relations resulting from that series

(Halisbury, 4th edition, Vol. 9, para 201, p80)

Contracts have been divided, according to the mode of their function, into three classes:

- Contracts of Record
- Contracts under seal
- Simple contracts

CHAPTER TWO

History of Contract Law

In this chapter, we will discuss briefly the history of contract law and its evolution. Having a climate where well defined contract laws exist and are protected by the state is essential for commerce to flourish in a country.

2.1 Contract Law in Roman Times

Roman law, codified by emperor Justinian in 6th century AD, had the concept of contracts.

They had three components of a valid contract namely, the thing which is contracted, the price of the thing and agreement or consent between the parties. The agreement could be in verbal or written form.

Roman law also allowed for different kinds of contracts including: sale-purchase, hire, partnership between two or more people and mandate or acting upon instructions. All types of contracts were enforceable by the law.

2.2 Contract law in the middle ages

In Europe in the middle ages, the contract law survived in an elementary form. However around 13th century as trade began to develop in Italian city states and elsewhere, the mercantile courts arose to resolve disputes between merchants on the basis of contract law.

2.3 Contracts under English common law

The English common law mainly was focused on the concept of debt, relating to a fixed sum of money owed that was recoverable, and the concept of covenant, relating to a promise made. In modern times, the common law version of contracts included offer, acceptance, consideration and the voluntary and mutual intent between the parties to be bound by the agreement.

2.4 Contracts under Canon law of the church

The Canon law of the catholic church in Europe during the middle ages also had a version of contracts. It had the notion that promises should be binding or *pacta sunt servanda* in Latin.

2.5 Contracts under Islamic law

Islamic law also had the notion of contracts. Under Islamic law, there were four elements of a contract namely the buyer, seller, subject matter of the contract (*maqud alayh*) and the form of the contract (*sighah*) comprising offer and acceptance. In India and the Arab world amd trading routes such as the silk route, an informal system of value transfer called the hawala system developed in the middle ages.

2.6 Contracts in British India

British India resulted in development of a court system based on common law, similar to the system in England. The main law governing contracts was the Indian Contract Act 1872.

2.7 Contract law in other countries

UK and its former colonies such as US, Canada and Australia follow the common law system, based on the legal precedents made by various courts.

In particular, different states of the USA may have a different set of precedents and hence slightly different versions or interpretations of the law. US follows a Uniform Commercial Code or UCC. Its contract law is based on the principles of an offer and acceptance of the offer, consideration for the offer and promissory estoppel which is the cause of action to decide when the contract is breached.

European countries like Germany generally follow the civil law system which is derived from the Roman law that was propounded by Emperor Justinian. Different countries in Europe have a common set of model rules called the Principles of European Contract Law (PECL), on which the contract laws of the individual countries are based.

2.8 Conclusion

In this chapter, we have briefly covered contract laws in different countries and cultures in history.

CHAPTER THREE

Indian Contract Act 1872

In this chapter we discuss the Indian Contract Act, which is the principal law in India that governs contracts. It was brought by the British rulers of India at that time and is based on similar laws in use in Britain.

3.1 Introduction to the Indian Contract Act 1872

THE INDIAN CONTRACT ACT, 1872

ACT NO. 9 OF 1872[1]

[25*th April*, 1872.]

Preamble—WHEREAS it is expedient to define and amend certain parts of the law relating to contracts;

It is hereby enacted as follows:—

PRELIMINARY

1. Short title.—This Act may be called the Indian Contract Act, 1872.

Extent, Commencement.—It extends to the whole of India [2][except the State of Jammu and Kashmir]; and it shall come into force on the first day of September, 1872.

Saving—[3]*** Nothing herein contained shall affect the provisions of any Statute, Act or Regulation not hereby expressly repealed, nor any usage or custom of trade, nor any incident of any contract, not inconsistent with the provisions of this Act.

2. Interpretation-clause.—In this Act the following words and expressions are used in the following senses, unless a contrary intention appears from the context:—

(*a*) When one person signifies to another his willingness to do or to abstain from doing anything, with a view to obtaining the assent of that other to such act or abstinence, he is said to make a proposal;

1. For the Statement of Objects and Reasons for the Bill which was based on a a report of Her Majesty's Commissioners appointed to prepare a body of substantive law for India, dated 6th July, 1866, *see* Gazette of India, 1867 Extraordinary, p. 34; for

Figure: First page of the Indian Contract Act 1872

The Indian Contract Act 1872 is the main act that defines the contract law in India. It states the circumstances in which a contract between two or more parties can be enforced in Indian law.

3.2 Elements of a Contract as per Indian Contract Act 1872

A legally binding contract must have the following elements, as per the Indian contract act 1872:

- **Offer**: There must be an offer by one party. The offer can be of different types such as:

a. express offer, that is made expressly in writing or through speech.
b. implied offer which is understood by the conduct of the parties.
c. general offer to the public or a specific offer to a party
d. continuous offer kept open for a time
e. counteroffer made by the person who is offered initially.

The offer should be in certain terms and not vague, may be written, spoken or implied, may be general or specific, continuous or time bound, and must be communicated. It should not just be a statement of intention. The offer may be revoked before acceptance, but once accepted it becomes legally binding. It can be rejected, either expressly or implied.

- **Acceptance**: The offer must be accepted by the other party. The law infers acceptance from certain actions, such as signing a contact or beginning to carry out the terms of a bargain.
- **Promise**: When the offer is accepted, it becomes a promise, which is legally enforceable.
- **Promisor and Promisee**: The person who makes the promise is called the promisor. The promise must be directed to a specific person, who accepts the promise and is called the promisee.
- **Consideration**: This refers to the price paid for the promise. In every valid contract, there must be an exchange of consideration. this means that something of value is given for something else of value. For example, if A buys a blouse at a store, A's consideration is the money being paid and the merchant's consideration is the item being bought. The value of the two items does not have to be the same, and law allows consumers to make both good deals and bad deals. As per the Indian Contract Act, a valid consideration exists when "*When at the desire of the promisor, the promisee or any other person has done or abstained from doing, or does or abstains from doing, or promises to do or abstain from*

doing something".

- **Agreement**: The promises made along with the consideration for the promise is called the agreement.
- **Contract**: An agreement enforceable by law is a contract.
- **Void contract**: A void contract is a contract that is not enforceable by law.
- People entering into a contract must be legally competent to make contracts. For example, they cannot be mentally ill or intoxicated, or less than the minimum age for contracts.
- **Performance**: This refers to the fulfilment of obligations by the parties as part of the contract.
- **Termination of a contract**: A contract can be terminated or discharged upon performance of the obligations, by mutual agreement between the parties, by lapse of time as per the Limitation Act, by death, insolvency, or alterations in the contract, or by breach of the contract.
- **Breach of a contract**: It is caused due to failure in performing the obligations by any party. The affected party can sue the party committing the breach in the court. Remedies available include damages, termination of the contract, specific performance of the contract or other remedies such as injunctions. Damages are typically awarded by the courts in such a way so as to restore the state as if the contract had been performed.

3.3 Acceptance as per the Indian Contract Act

The rules for acceptance of a contract as per the Indian Contract Act are as follows:

- **Absolute and unqualified**: Acceptance of an offer by a party should be absolute and unqualified. For example, there should not be a counteroffer by the party to buy the items at a different price than that one offered
- **Communicated**: The acceptance should be communicated to the party making the offer, in a written or verbal form.
- **Mode**: Acceptance must be in the mode prescribed. If not, the offerer may inform the same to the person accepting the offer that the acceptance is not as per the prescribed mode such as writing or verbal or email.

- **Time frame**: The acceptance must be made within a specific time frame and before the offer is lapsed.
- **Acceptance after offer**: The acceptance can only be after an offer is made, not earlier.
- Silence by one party cannot be held as acceptance.
- Acceptance must be given expressly by speech or in writing, or else implied by the actions of the acceptor of the offer.
- Acceptance should be of all the terms of the offer, not just some of the terms.

3.4 Lawful consideration as per the Indian Contract Act

The rules for lawful consideration as per the Indian Contract Act include the following:

- The action should be at the desire or request of the promisor. If the action has been made without the promisor expressly requesting for it, then no consideration is payable.
- The consideration must be real and not illusory.
- The consideration must be having some value as per law.
- Consideration may be in the past, present or future.
- Consideration may move from the promisee to another person.
- Consideration need not be adequate or equal in value to something given. All that is necessary is that it should have some value.

The rules for unlawful consideration are as follows:

- Consideration must not be something that the promiser is already bound to do.
- Consideration should not be forbidden by law
- Consideration should not involve injury to any person
- Consideration should not be immoral, fraudulent, or opposed to public policy

3.5 Persons competent to make contracts as per the Indian Contract Act

The persons competent to make a contract include the following:

- The person should not be a minor as per law.

- They should not be bankrupt.
- They should not be of unsound mind when making the contract, such as mentally ill or intoxicated.
- They should not be disqualified by law from making the contract, such as being a convict, or alien enemy.
- They should be making the contract out of their own free will and consent, and not be subject to coercion, undue influence, fraud or misrepresentation.

3.6 Performance as per Indian Contract Act

Performance of a contract is the fulfilment of the obligations. Performance can be immediate or delayed or time bound, can be performed by one party or be reciprocal, and can be demanded by the party to whom the obligation is promised or by their heirs or legal representatives.

Section 37 of the Contract Act states as follows: *Obligation of parties to contract.—The parties to a contract must either perform, or offer to perform, their respective promises, unless such performance is dispensed with or excused under the provisions of this Act, or of any other law. —The parties to a contract must either perform, or offer to perform, their respective promises, unless such performance is dispensed with or excused under the provisions of this Act, or of any other law." Promises bind the representatives of the promisors in case of the death of such promisors before performance, unless a contrary intention appears from the contract.*

3.7 Agency

As per the law, the contracts can be made either between the two parties directly, or by the persons (the agents) who are legally authorized and competent to act on behalf of the parties (the principals).

The agency can come to an end in any of the following ways:

- If the principal revokes the agency of the agent
- If the agent themselves renounce their agency
- If the business of the agent is completed
- If the principal is declared insolvent.

3.9 Conclusion

In this chapter, we have gone through the basic elements of the Indian Contract Act 1872. In the following chapters we shall discuss some specific cases related to the act in more detail.

CHAPTER FOUR

Fraud, Coercion and Undue Influence in Contracts

In this chapter we discuss the conditions that constitute fraud, coercion or undue influence in a contract. If any of these conditions are proven, the contract can be voided.

4.1 Fraud in a contract

Some definitions of fraud from dictionaries and judgments are as follows:

- A fraud is an act of deliberate deception with the design of securing something by taking unfair advantage of another. It is the deception in order to gain by another's loss. It is a cheating intended to get an advantage [SP Chengalvanya v Jagannath AIR 1994 SC 853].
- Fraud arises out of a deliberate active role of representation about a fact which he knows to be untrue, yet he succeeds in misleading the representee by making him believe it to be true. The representation to become fraudulent must be of fact made with the knowledge that it was false [Shristi v Shaw Bros. AIR 1992 SC 1555].
- Fraud is a false misrepresentation by one who is aware that it was untrue with an intention to mislead the other who may act upon it to his prejudice and to the advantage of the representator [State of Maharashtra v Buddhikota AIR 1989 SC 2292].

- Webster's third New International Dictionary - Fraud in equity has been defined as an act or omission to act or concealment by which one person obtains an advantage against conscience over another or which equity or public policy forbids as being prejudicial to another.

- Black's law dictionary – fraud is defined as an intentional perversion of truth for the purpose of inducing another in reliance upon it to part with some valuable thing belonging to him or surrender a legal right; a false representation of a matter of fact whether by words or conduct, by false or misleading allegations, or by concealment of that which should have been disclosed, which deceives and is intended to deceive another so that he shall act upon it to his legal injury.
- Halisbury laws of England – a representation is deemed to have been false and therefore a misrepresentation, if it was at the material date false in substance and in fact.

Although it is not exactly correct to say that fraud must be proved with strictures of a criminal charge, there is no doubt that a very high degree of proof is needed to establish it [William and Mortimer 16th Ed p 173].

Fraud, in all cases, implies a willful act on the part of anyone whereby, another is sought to be deprived by illegal or inequitable means, of something which he is entitled to [Green v Nixon (1857) 23 Bear 530].

Fraud has been defined in Section 17 of the Contract Act which is but an explanation.

Fraud is either actual or constructive. Actual fraud is sub divided into two parts:

- misrepresentation and
- concealment.

Misrepresentation (called *suggestio falsi*) must be of a material fact and must have been relied or acted upon by the person deceived.

Concealment (called *suppresio veri*) is the suppression or withholding of some material fact, being some fact which one party was under the legal duty to the other to disclose [Turner v Green (1895) 2 CH 205, AIR 1953 SC 163, AIR 1956 MB 246, 249].

Effect of fraud: the effect of fraud on any processing or transaction is that it becomes a nullity. Even the most solemn proceedings stand vitiated if they are actuated by fraud. Such being the nature and consequence of it, the law requires not only strict pleading of it but strict proof as well.

If fraud is proved in a contract, the affected party can make it void, or apply for damages from the party that committed fraud, or can insist of the performance of the original contract.

4.2 Coercion in a contract

Compulsion by physical force or threat of physical force, conduct that constitutes the improper use of economic power to compel another to submit to the wishes of one who wields it [Black's Law Dictionary].

Coercion takes an infinite number of forms, but it may properly be thus defined: the moment that the person who influences the other does so by the threat of taking away from that other something that he then possesses, or by preventing him from obtaining an advantage he would otherwise have obtained, then it becomes coercion and ceases to be persuasion or consideration [Ellis v Barker (1871) 40 LJ Ch 603/607].

Coercion is defined by Section 15 of the Contract Act 1872 as "the committing or threatening to commit any act forbidden by law (IPC) or the unlawful deterring or threatening to detain any property to the prejudice of any person whatever with the intention of causing any person to enter into an agreement." It is the first portion of the definition which would properly apply. To constitute undue influence in the eyes of the law, there must be coercion.

Examples of coercion are as follows:

- Threat to commit suicide is coercion [AIR 1969 Cal 293].
- Coercion in Section 72 of the Contract Act must be understood in the ordinary sense. In includes every kind of compulsion even if it does not measure up to the definition under Section 15 of the Contract Act [AIR 1969 MYS 230]

4.3 Undue Influence in a Contract

Undue influence is the improper use of power or trust in a way that deprives a person of free will and substitutes another's objective [Black's Law Dictionary: 8th Edition].

Undue influence includes any influence in which the exercise of free and deliberate judgement is excluded. Undue influence is presumed until the contrary is proved when the relation of the parties is such that one is entitled to the confidential advice of the other, as in the case of solicitor and client, of a trustee and trust and of a parent contracting with a child who has first come of age. In other cases of confidential relationship, the party seeking to avoid a contract must prove undue influence [Sutton and Shannon on Contracts 6th Edition].

Every influence cannot be characterized as undue. A done can appeal and persuade the donor to make a gift to him. Such appeals and persuasions cannot be characterized as undue influence, provided the donor retains the mental capacity [Takri Devi v Rama AIR 1984 HP 11, 15, Subhas v Ganga Prasad AIR 1967 SC 878, Afsar v Solamn AIR 1976 SC 163].

When the will of the testator is coerced into doing that which he or she does not intend to do, it is undue influence [Boudams v Richardson (1906) AC 169].

Undue influence as defined in Section 16 of the Contract Act 1872, is that relation which subsists between the parties by which one of the parties is in a position to dominate the will of the other and uses that position to obtain an unfair advantage over that other [AIR 1996 Ker 64, AIR 1956 MB 246, AIR 1960 Cal 551, AIR 1979 SC 1431, Barry and Butler – AIR 1976 Cal 377, AIR 1955 SC 363, AIR 1968 SC 964].

Undue influence is 'coercion' only if it takes away the free agency of the testator. Whatever takes away the free agency of the testator, constitutes coercion [11 CWN 824].

CHAPTER FIVE

Void and Voidable Contracts

In this chapter we discuss the conditions that make a contract invalid or unenforceable as per the Indian contract act. If these rules are met then the contract is considered void or cannot be enforced.

5.1 Conditions for void or unenforceable contracts

Agreements to do something illegal or something that is against public policy are not enforceable in the courts and are hence considered void. For example, an agreement to sell illegal drugs.

A minor person usually cannot enter into a contract. E.g., a person under the age of 18 for male and 21 for female is a minor and cannot enter into a contract.

A contract that is unfair e.g., which favors a particular party may be found unfair and unconscionable, and hence unenforceable in the court if the following conditions are met:

- the consumer is presented with a contract on a take it or leave it basis.
- there is uneven bargaining power between the parties, such as when the seller is educated and experienced and the consumer is uneducated.

Some types of work bonds, such as a promise to work in an IT company for a certain number of years or to never work for a competitor, may also be unenforceable.

Fraud and misrepresentation are grounds for invalidating a contract. An example of a fraud is a false statement to induce one party to agree to a contract. Misrepresentation can be in the form of either making a misleading statement or intentionally withholding information in a statement that could have caused the party to not agree to the contract.

Some other types of void contracts are as follows:

- **Mistake of fact**: If there are mistakes in the contract that are factually wrong, that can make it void.
- **Mistake of law**: If the consideration or the object of the contract is illegal, that can make the contract void. However, part of the contract may still be valid.
- **Agreements without Consideration**: A contract without consideration is void.
- **Agreements in restraint of trade**: A contract that restrains trade are void since they infringe on the free choice of the persons.
- **Agreements in restraint of marriage**: Such agreements are also void since they infringe of person's freedom, these apply for contracts that restrain the right of a person to marry another.
- **Agreements in restraint of legal proceedings** are also deemed void.
- **Uncertainty or Impossibility of performance**: Contracts involving actions that are impossible to perform are also deemed as void.
- Agreements related to wagers and bets are also deemed as void.

5.2 Voidable contracts

Some contracts are voidable, means they can be rendered void by any of the parties. Until they are rendered void, they remain valid and enforceable. This includes cases such as the following:

- **Lack of free consent**: This may happen where one of the parties may not have given consent out of free will. Therefore, if one of the parties can prove they were coerced into making the contract, they can choose to void it.
- **Prevention of performance by the other party:** If it is proved that the other party has prevented the party from fulfilling its performance obligations then the contract can be voided by the party which was prevented.

5.3 Conclusion

In this chapter we have considered some conditions that can void the contract absolutely, or where one of the parties can choose to void it if the conditions for voidability are met.

CHAPTER SIX

Quasi Contracts

In this chapter, we discuss the concept of quasi contracts as defined in the Indian Contract Act.

6.1 Introduction to Quasi-Contracts

These are not pure contracts but relations that resemble some elements of a contract. The Indian contract Act Chapter 5 covers quasi-contracts. These are obligations from one party to another even though they have not entered into a formal contract. These can constitute when a benefit has been received by one party at the expense of another party, and the benefit received is unjust.

Some examples of quasi-contracts include the following:

- Necessities received by a party who is not eligible or incapable of getting into a contract, such as a lunatic or minor person. An example can be some life-saving medicines or other necessities received by a severely ill or disabled person, who is obliged to pay for them.
- Reimbursement of an amount of money, or arrears, paid by one party to another.
- Enjoyment of some goods of services that are not done gratuitously as a gift.
- Where a party has dropped or misplaced some goods and they have been found by another party, who has the responsibility to return them to the rightful owner.

A benefit obtained by a party by mistake or coercion. An example can be a bank transfer done by mistake to a wrong account.

CHAPTER SEVEN

Warranty

In this chapter we discuss the concept of warranty as a contract or part of a contract.

7.1 Introduction to Warranty

Warranty is a type of contract, or one or more conditions present in a contract. A warranty is a promise or guarantee made by a seller concerning the quality or performance of goods offered for sale. It is usually valid for a limited time period. A warranty is a statement of what the seller will do to fix any defect in the product, or if it does not perform as advertised, within the time period of its validity. If the seller does not honor the warranty, the contract is said to be breached.

The sale of goods act 1930 states the flowing:

13. When condition to be treated as warranty.—

(1) Where a contract of sale is subject to any condition to be fulfilled by the seller, the buyer may waive the condition or elect to treat the breach of the condition as a breach of warranty and not as a ground for treating the contract as repudiated.

(2) Where a contract of sale is not severable and the buyer has accepted the goods or part thereof, the breach of any condition to be fulfilled by the seller can only be treated as a breach of warranty and not as a ground for rejecting the goods and treating the contract as repudiated, unless there is a term of the contract, express or implied, to that effect.

(3) Nothing in this section shall affect the case of any condition or warranty fulfilment of which is excused by law by reason of impossibility or otherwise.

7.2 Types of warranties

There are two types of warranties: express and implied.

- **Express warranty**: it is an express statement concerning the quality or performance of goods for sale that is part of the contract of sale.

- **Implied warranty**: this is understood by the conduct of the seller to the buyer of the goods.

In the following chapter, we look at another law in India related to contracts for sale of goods.

CHAPTER EIGHT

Sale of Goods Act 1930

In this chapter we discuss the Sale of Goods Act, that defines the law in India related to the sale of goods. It is another law that was introduced in British India and reflects the similar law in Britain of the time.

8.1 Introduction to the Sale of Goods Act 1930

Sale of Goods Act of 1930 defines the law related to the sale of goods and transfer of ownership, including moveable property but not land.

It mainly focuses on contracts between the buyers and sellers.

THE SALE OF GOODS ACT, 1930

ACT NO. 3 OF 1930[1]

[15*th March*, 1930.]

An Act to define and amend the law relating to the sale of goods.

WHEREAS it is expedient to define and amend the law relating to the sale of goods; It is hereby enacted as follows:—

CHAPTER I

PRELIMINARY

1. Short title, extent and commencement.—(*1*) This Act may be called the [2]*** Sale of Goods Act, 1930.

[3][(*2*) It extends to the whole of India [4][except the State of Jammu and Kashmir].]

(*3*) It shall come into force on the 1st day of July, 1930.

2. Definitions.—In this Act, unless there is anything repugnant in the subject or context,—

(*1*) "buyer" means a person who buys or agrees to buy goods;

(*2*) "delivery" means voluntary transfer of possession from one person to another;

(*3*) goods are said to be in a "deliverable state" when they are in such state that the buyer would under the contract be bound to take delivery of them;

(*4*) "document of title to goods" includes a bill of lading, dockwarrant, warehouse keeper's certificate, wharfingers' certificate, railway receipt, [5][multimodal transport document,] warrant or order for the delivery of goods and any other document used in the ordinary course of business as proof of the possession or control of goods, or authorising or purporting to authorise, either by endorsement or by delivery, the possessor of the document to transfer or receive goods thereby

Figure: First page of the Sale of Goods Act 1930

8.2 Contract under sale of goods act

The Sale of Goods Act 1930 defines a contract for a sale of goods between a buyer and a seller, where the ownership of an item is transferred from the seller to the buyer upon payment of a price.

The term goods refers to "*every kind of movable property other than actionable claims and money; and includes stock and shares, growing crops, grass, and things attached to or forming part of the land which are agreed to be severed before sale or under the contract of sale.*"

8.3 Transfer of risks and liabilities

Along with the ownership and rights, any risks and liabilities associated with the item are also transferred from the seller to the buyer. the act covers existing goods as well as goods to be transferred in the future.

The Sale of Goods act defines what is a contract of sale and the various conditions associated with the contract. It also covers various cases where the goods are faulty or the contract conditions are not met. It covers the rights of the buyers and the sellers, as well as special conditions like damaged goods and auctions.

CHAPTER NINE

Conclusion

In this book, we have discussed what is a contract and the laws in India related to contracts, particularly the Indian Contract Act 1872 and its elements. We have also briefly discussed the sale of goods act, that covers conditions related to sale of goods.

We have discussed the various elements of a contract and how a contract can be voided. We have also discussed some special types of contracts such as warranties and obligations created by quasi contracts.

As mentioned, a strong contract law whose terms are enforced is essential for the development of a free market in trade and commerce in any country. The Indian Contract Act serves to fill such a demand in India.

It is hoped that this book might help people to become familiar with contract law in India.

About The Author

Siva Prasad Bose has authored more than twenty introductory guidebooks related to aspects of Indian laws in Hindi and English. He is currently retired after many years of service in Uttar Pradesh Power Corporation Limited. He received his engineering degree from Jadavpur University, Kolkata, has a law degree from Meerut University, Meerut and Bachelor of Science degree from MMH College in Ghaziabad.

His interests lie in the fields of family law, civil law, law of contracts, and areas of law related to electricity generation and revenue related issues.

Other Books By Siva Prasad Bose

Introduction to Wills and Probate
Senior Citizens Abuse in India
Introduction to Negotiable Instruments
Introduction to Marriage Laws in India
Neighbor Problems in India and what to do about them
Managing Court Cases with Mental Strength
Delays in Court Cases in India
Self-Publish Books and E-Books in India
Introduction to Patents and Patent Law in India
Introduction to Property Law in India

Printed by Libri Plureos GmbH in Hamburg,
Germany